IT'LL NEVER
WORK
WEAPONS
AND WARFARE

JON RICHARDS

W
FRANKLIN WATTS
LONDON·SYDNEY

Franklin Watts
First published in Great Britain in 2016 by
The Watts Publishing Group

Copyright © The Watts Publishing
Group, 2016

Credits
Conceived, designed and edited by
Tall Tree Ltd
Series Editor: Rob Colson
Series Designer: Gary Hyde

ISBN 978 1 4451 5030 7

Printed in China

Franklin Watts
An imprint of
Hachette Children's Group
Part of The Watts Publishing Group
Carmelite House
50 Victoria Embankment
London EC4Y 0DZ

An Hachette UK Company
www.hachette.co.uk

www.franklinwatts.co.uk

Picture credits:
t-top, b-bottom, l-left, r-right,
c-centre, m-middle
All images public domain unless
otherwise indicated:
Front cover Dreamstime.com/Jens Stolt, Dreamstime.
com/Bevanward, 3b Dreamstime.com/Michael Gray, 4c
Dreamstime.com/Jens Stolt 4bl Dreamstime.com/Ken
Backer 4bl Dreamstime.com/Woverwolf, 5br
Dreamstime.com/Zim235, 6c Dreamstime.com/Rafael
Laguillo, 10cl Dreamstime.com/Cdonofrio, 11t
Dreamstime.com/Smontgom65, 12c Dreamstime.com/
Meunierd, 13br Dreamstime.com/Maro Faccio, 13c
Dreamstime.com/Michael Gray, 14b Dreamstime.com/
Gary Blakeley, 16b Dreamstime.com/Bevanward, 17b
Dreamstime.com/Val Armstrong, 22tDreamstime.com/
Elena Duvernay

CONTENTS

HAND-HELD WEAPONS

Since the earliest times, humans have carried weapons. Axes and clubs were used for hunting and for fighting, but for centuries the most important weapon was the sword.

STONE-AGE WEAPONS

The first weapons were made from flint, a type of rock that will break with sharp edges when hit with another rock. These weapons were first used to kill animals for food. Sharpened flint heads were tied to sticks to make axes or to long wooden shafts to make spears.

Sharp flint axe head

Bronze Egyptian sword

Iron Phoenician sword (Middle East)

Bronze Chinese double-edged sword

METAL BLADES

The Stone Age ended about 6,000 years ago when people started to use metal to make tools and weapons. This was the start of the Bronze Age. Bronze, a mix of copper and tin, was easier to shape than stone and created a sharper edge. It could also be shaped into long swords. People started to use iron and steel to make weapons from about 1200 BCE. Steel is a strong mix of iron and carbon. A steel sword could even pierce the medieval metal armour shown opposite.

SAMURAI SWORD

Swords used by noble Japanese warriors, or samurai, were called katana, and they are considered the finest of all swords. From about CE 800, swordsmiths began making blades from layers of different types of steel that were folded over and over to remove impurities and to create an incredibly strong metal. The blade was polished for up to three weeks using fine stone grains to create a razor-sharp edge.

The samurai carried two katana.

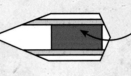

Combining soft and hard steel made a katana strong and flexible.

A medieval longsword was made from steel.

Armour plating was also made from steel.

MODERN SWORDS

Following the development of modern firearms, including rifles (see pages 10–11), swords are now used only during military and police ceremonies, where they are worn as part of a uniform. However, sharp blades called bayonets are still part of a soldier's equipment, and are fitted to the ends of rifles to create stabbing weapons.

Bayonet on the end of an assault rifle

CATAPULTS, SPEARS, ARROWS

While swords allowed warriors to fight an enemy face-to-face, a weapon they could throw allowed them to attack from a distance.

👉 1. SPEARS

Spears could be thrust or thrown. Early spears used stone points, but these were replaced by bronze tips from about 3000 BCE. Roman soldiers in the first century BCE used a type of spear called a *pilum*. Its iron shaft was designed to bend once it had been thrown so it was hard to pull out of the body and couldn't be used by the enemy.

Roman legionary carrying a pilum.

After it was used, the shaft of the pilum would bend.

SPEAR THROWERS

From the 14th century, the Aztecs perfected the art of spear-throwing using the atlatl, *a device that had been in use since the Stone Age. This was a shaft with a groove at one end into which the spear was fixed. The* atlatl *increased the speed the spear could leave the thrower and the distance it could travel.*

A spear-thrower using an atlatl.

BOWS AND ARROWS 👉

In medieval warfare, there were two main types of bow. The crossbow featured a horizontal bow and fired short bolts. Crossbows were very powerful, and could be used by regular soldiers without special training. However, they were slow to reload. Longbows were held vertically, and shot longer arrows. They were faster to reload, but needed skill to master. In the hands of a trained bowman, however, they could be used to devastating effect.

English longbowmen defeat the French at the Battle of Crécy in 1346.

Crossbows were so deadly that in 1139 the Catholic Church tried to ban them.

LAYING SIEGE

Catapults were large weapons designed to hurl missiles at enemy troops and positions. These missiles could be large metal bolts, huge pieces of rock or even the bodies of infected animals or people, launched with the aim of spreading disease among enemy troops. Early catapults were used by the ancient Greeks and Romans 2,000 years ago. Over time, these powerful machines increased in size and strength, culminating with the huge medieval trebuchets.

A 13th-century Mongol trebuchet

BIG GUNS

Cannons were invented in China in the 14th century and spread through the Middle East to Europe. They used gunpowder to fire enormous shells that could smash fortified walls.

THE TSAR CANNON

A bombard was an early cannon that fired a large metal or stone ball. This giant bombard was made in Russia in 1586. The inside of the barrel measured 89 centimetres across. However, the cannon was only ever fired once and never used in battle.

The Tsar Cannon proved too big to use.

Little David, ready to fire

LITTLE DAVID

This US cannon was built towards the end of the Second World War (1939–1945). It was designed to be assembled in 12 hours, while other cannons of a similar size would need up to three weeks to set in place. However, tests showed that it wasn't very accurate and the war ended before it could be used.

A shell fired by Little David

SUPER-CANNONS 👉

Large weapons that fire shells over long distances are called artillery. Normal artillery uses a single charge of powder to blast a shell. This limits the shell's range to the amount of powder that will fit into it. Towards the end of the Second World War, German forces developed the V-3 cannon, which used a series of smaller charges to blast a shell over huge distances. It was aimed at London from special bunkers in Calais in France – about 150 kilometres. However, Allied bombing destroyed the bunkers before the cannons could be used, and the Allied invasion of D-Day in 1944 pushed the cannons beyond the range of England.

Barrel

The V-3's barrel shaft passed up a hill. Multiple charges along the shaft boosted the shell's speed.

Test-firing the M777 howitzer.

MODERN ARTILLERY

The latest US army artillery equipment has computerised firing systems. The M777 howitzer can hit targets up to 40 kilometres away. It is made from the lightweight metal titanium and can be transported by helicopter or lorry. While older models needed a crew of nine to operate them, the M777 can be operated by just five soldiers. In 2012, the M777 was used in Afghanistan to fire at a target that was 35 kilometres away, the longest artillery shot in the history of the US Marine Corps.

SMALL ARMS

Gunpowder had been used in warfare since the 14th century, but it wasn't until the 17th century in Europe that small hand-held gunpowder firearms called muskets were used.

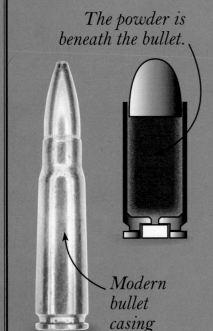

The powder is beneath the bullet.

Modern bullet casing

HOW FIREARMS WORK

The first practical firearms worked in much the same way as cannons. Powder in the barrel exploded with such force that it blasted a bullet out of the barrel. While the earliest bullets had separate powder and shot, a modern bullet has the shot and powder contained within a single casing. Early firearms were fired by setting the powder alight with a burning wick or the spark from a flint. This method was unreliable, especially if the powder was damp. Modern bullets have a primer at the bottom of the casing, which ignites the powder when it is hit by a firing pin.

RIFLED BARREL

Early firearms were very inaccurate because the bullets became unstable once they were flying through the air. The solution was to carve spirals, called rifling, into the gun's barrel. These made the bullets spin as they flew, allowing them to travel in a straight line.

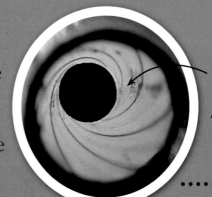

Rifling in the barrel gives rifles their name.

17th-century instructions for firing a musket

THE MUSKET 👉

One of the earliest types of firearm was the musket. This long weapon was loaded through the muzzle, with gunpowder, a metal ball, or shot, and wadding to keep everything in place. The loading process was laborious and even the most skilled soldiers could only fire up to four shots a minute.

Lead musket balls

The musket was a common weapon until the 19th century.

MODERN RIFLES 👈

Today's assault rifles are very powerful and can fire hundreds of bullets a minute. They have cases called magazines, which can hold 30-50 bullets, allowing a soldier to fire many times without reloading. However, these improvements still haven't prevented problems. When first introduced in the Vietnam War in the 1960s, the M16 rifle often jammed, because it came with inadequate cleaning materials. An improved model with a new barrel reduced jamming. As a result, the M16 remained the main infantry weapon of US forces until the 1990s.

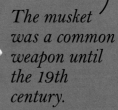

The new, improved M16

EARLY ARMOUR

The body armour soldiers have worn has taken many forms, from the earliest thick leather vests to today's bullet- and blast-proof shielding. However, the design of all armour has needed to balance protection with ease of movement.

EARLY ARMOUR

The first armour was made from thick padded cloth, stiffened leather or even plates of wood. These were later replaced by thin, overlapping strips of metal. These were light, but could restrict movement.

Roman steel segmented armour

CHAINMAIL

Much heavier but easier to wear was an armour using small metal loops, linked together to create chainmail. The interlocking rings were very good at deflecting sharp objects, such as swords and spears, but not so good at reducing the impact of a club. To reduce injury, soldiers wore thick padded clothes beneath the armour to absorb blows.

11th-century soldiers in chainmail

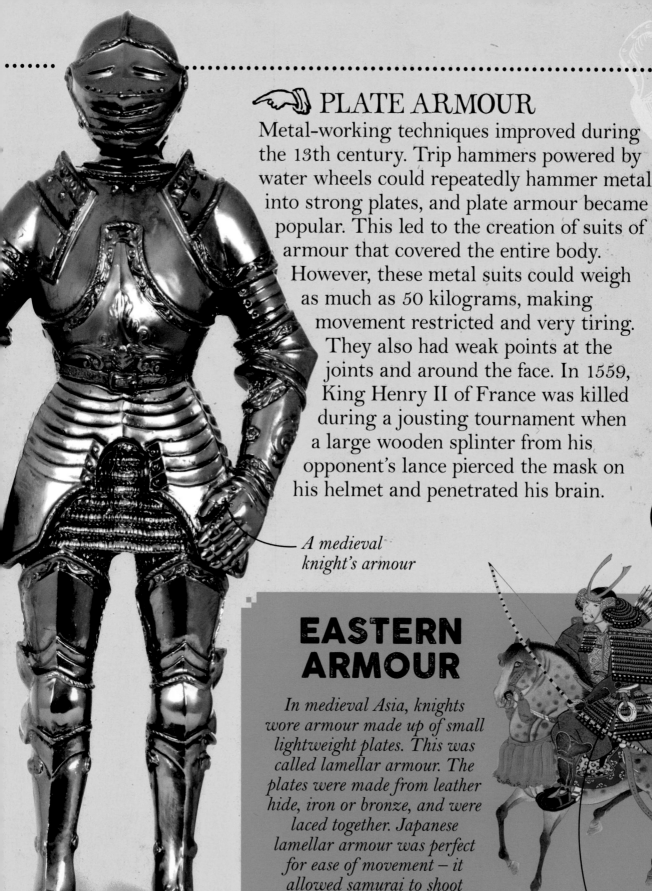

☞ PLATE ARMOUR

Metal-working techniques improved during the 13th century. Trip hammers powered by water wheels could repeatedly hammer metal into strong plates, and plate armour became popular. This led to the creation of suits of armour that covered the entire body. However, these metal suits could weigh as much as 50 kilograms, making movement restricted and very tiring. They also had weak points at the joints and around the face. In 1559, King Henry II of France was killed during a jousting tournament when a large wooden splinter from his opponent's lance pierced the mask on his helmet and penetrated his brain.

A medieval knight's armour

EASTERN ARMOUR

In medieval Asia, knights wore armour made up of small lightweight plates. This was called lamellar armour. The plates were made from leather hide, iron or bronze, and were laced together. Japanese lamellar armour was perfect for ease of movement – it allowed samurai to shoot arrows, ride on horseback and fight with swords.

A samurai in lamellar armour

MODERN ARMOUR

Today's soldiers still wear armour as part of their battle dress. It must be strong enough to protect them against modern weapons.

FIRST WORLD WAR ARMOUR ☞

During the First World War (1914–1918), the Germans developed armour made from nickel and silicon plates. Nicknamed 'lobster armour', as the layers resembled the body of a lobster, it protected against pistol rounds and bayonets, but not against more powerful guns.

German 'lobster armour' from 1918

HELMETS

For thousands of years, soldiers wore heavy metal helmets to protect their heads in battle. Today's soldiers wear lightweight helmets made of a super-strong material called Kevlar, which protects against bullets or bomb blasts. Kevlar is a synthetic fibre invented by US chemist Stephanie Kwolek in 1965. It is five times stronger than steel.

Bronze ancient Greek helmet

Steel medieval helmet

Kevlar US army helmet

BULLETPROOF

From the 17th century, wars were increasingly fought with guns, so soldiers needed protection from bullets. Early bulletproof armour was made of steel and was heavy to wear. In the 19th century, a lightweight bulletproof vest made from layers of silk was invented, but it was extremely expensive. Modern bulletproof vests are made from Kevlar and are much more effective.

Testing a silk bulletproof vest in 1923.

US Navy troops in modern armour

☞ I. MODERN ARMOUR

The armour worn by today's soldiers is designed to absorb and disperse the energy of a bullet. It is light and flexible to allow the soldiers to move freely, and is often covered in camouflage patterns to conceal the wearer from the enemy.

15

BOMB DISPOSAL ☞

Perhaps the most extreme form of modern armour is worn by bomb disposal experts. These bomb suits have overlapping parts, made from layers of Kevlar, plastic and foam, which cover the body, protecting the wearer from a potential blast and any shrapnel. The suits can weigh nearly 40 kilograms, but have saved the lives of bomb disposal experts.

A German bomb-disposal expert

ANIMALS IN WARFARE

Whether it's for their physical strength, speed or ability to reach places people can't, animals have been used in battle to carry weapons or as weapons themselves, sometimes with disastrous consequences.

THE HORSE

The most successful animal ever used in warfare is the horse. For centuries, horses carried soldiers into battle. In fact, the largest contiguous empire the world has ever seen – stretching from China to Europe – was conquered in the 13th century by Mongol armies on horseback. The Mongols used a small, fast breed of horse, and were skilled at shooting arrows as they rode.

Mongol ruler Genghis Khan (1162–1227)

WAR ELEPHANTS 👉

These huge animals charged at the enemy, spreading mayhem. First used in India in about 2000 BCE, their use spread to Europe after Alexander the Great saw them in action in India in 331 BCE. However, elephants could scare easily. In a battle between Greeks and Megarans in 226 BCE, elephants fled in terror from pigs that had been doused in oil and set alight.

Alexander the Great rides into battle on a war elephant.

Soviet military dog training school

👈 ANTI-TANK DOGS

During the Second World War, the Soviet Red Army trained dogs to carry bombs under enemy tanks (see pages 18–19), where the bombs would explode. However, the Soviets used their own diesel-fuel tanks to train the dogs, rather than petrol ones as used by the Germans. The dogs ran beneath the familiar Soviet tanks, rather than German ones, with disastrous results!

17

BAT BOMBS

In the middle of the Second World War, US forces came up with an idea to use bats against Japan. By strapping small bombs to the bats and throwing them from planes, the Americans hoped the creatures would fly into the eaves of houses, where the bombs would explode and spread fires. However, the plan was scrapped in 1943 after the bats set fire to their own military base, where they had been released by accident!

EARLY TANKS

A tank is a heavily armoured vehicle that provides protection and firepower to troops on the battlefield. The first practical tanks were made in the early 20th century.

EARLY DESIGN

Italian inventor Leonardo da Vinci created a design for a tank in 1487. His vehicle had sloping sides to deflect missiles, and cannons pointing out from its edges. It would have had difficulty moving due to its size and weight. It was never built, but the idea of the tank was born. Not until 1899 did an army see the need for an armoured vehicle. The British built a 'motor war car' that was 28 metres long and fitted with two machine guns, but it was never tested in battle.

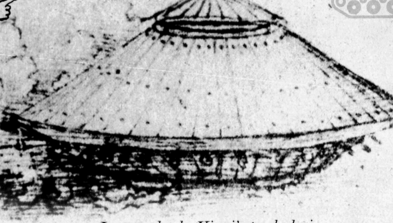

Leonardo da Vinci's tank design

A British motor war car of 1902

THE 'WATER' TANK

During the First World War, the British created a vehicle to roll across enemy trenches. To keep it a secret as it was developed, the project was referred to as a 'water tank', and the 'tank' name has since stuck. The Mark I tank first saw action in 1916. This early tank was dangerous as the fuel tank was located above the crew – a direct hit could empty burning fuel onto them. The Mark IV tank of 1917 moved the fuel tank to a less dangerous position.

The Mark IV was safer and more heavily armed than the Mark I.

TSAR TANK

This experimental Russian tank of 1915 featured two huge bicycle wheels at the front, which measured 9 metres across. The cabin and weapons were suspended between these, while at the rear was a single, small wheel that was just 1.5 metres across. During its first test runs, the tank's small rear wheel got stuck in mud. It was abandoned where it stood and no others were made.

The tank's huge wheels made it an easy target

MODERN TANKS

By the start of the Second World War, tanks had taken on the standard design that is still in use today, with caterpillar tracks supporting a body and a rotating gun turret on top.

Rotating flail to detonate mines

Turret

An American Sherman tank

Caterpillar tracks

FUNNY TANKS

On 6 June 1944, Allied forces invaded France in a campaign to liberate Europe from Nazi rule. To help achieve this, engineers created tanks known as funny tanks. One had a large rotating flail fitted to the front. This was designed to detonate buried land mines. Another had a large bundle of wood, called a fascine, strapped to the tank. This was dropped into a trench to allow the tank to roll over it. Sometimes the flail threw up so much dust that the driver couldn't see, or the fascine would be crushed or float away.

Tank with fascine

AMPHIBIOUS TANKS

DD (Duplex Drive) tanks were designed to 'swim' ashore from ships during the Second World War. They were fitted with a canvas skirt, which could be pulled up to make the tank float. However, many of the tanks sank as they encountered rough seas. The modern amphibious (swimming) Leopard tank can be fitted with a large snorkel. This is a tall metal pipe that sticks above the water's surface while the tank drives across the bottom. The pipe lets air into the tank and also gives the tank commander a good vantage point.

The commander stands at the top of a Leopard tank's snorkel.

MODERN BATTLE TANKS

Tank designs have adapted to the dangers of the modern battlefield. Their bodies are as low to the ground as possible to flatten the tank's shape, making it a harder target to hit. The turret is also low and its sloped sides are designed to deflect incoming shells. The whole tank is covered in thick armour to protect it against today's powerful explosives. Many tanks can also be sealed shut and have their own air supply in the event of a nuclear or chemical attack.

An Israeli Merkava tank fires a shell.

SINKING SHIPS

The first warships carried soldiers to board and capture enemy vessels, and to ram and sink other warships. From the 14th century, ships were armed with cannons, becoming floating gun platforms that fired shells at enemy ships.

RAMMING SPEED!

By the 5th century BCE, Greek warships were slender wooden galleys designed to ram enemy ships. A metal spike fitted to the prow would punch a hole in an enemy ship's hull and sink it. These ships had sails, but relied on muscle power for their ramming speed. A ship with two rows of oars was called a bireme and one with three rows was called a trireme.

Metal spike in the prow of a trireme.

Triremes were light enough to be carried ashore by the crew.

A Viking longship used sails and oarsmen.

VIKING LONGSHIP

In the 8th century CE, Vikings raided Europe in narrow boats called longships. The longship was light and fast. It could sail across seas and up shallow rivers to surprise the enemy.

MARY ROSE 👉

By the 16th century, warships used elaborate sails, rather than rowers. However, the larger ships could be unstable. After 30 years' service, the *Mary Rose*, flagship of King Henry VIII of England, was refitted. Newer, heavier guns were added. As the ship left port in 1545, a gust of wind tilted the ship while the gunports were open. Water rushed in and the ship sank.

The Mary Rose *was fitted with 91 guns.*

ROUND SHIP

By the latter half of the 19th century, warships were made largely from metal and were powered by steam engines. The Russian warship Novgorod, launched in 1874, was round in shape. It was designed to provide a stable gun platform, and to sail in shallow water. However, its shape made the ship very slow and inefficient – it took about 45 minutes to turn a full circle. Eventually, the ship was used as a floating fort before becoming a store ship.

An overhead view of the Novgorod

ON AND UNDER WATER

As ironclad ships replaced wooden ships, navies needed more than ships with guns – they needed floating air force bases and submarines.

ARMOURED WARSHIPS

All-metal ships, called ironclads, were built from the 1850s. The French ship *La Gloire* and the British ship HMS *Warrior* were the first ironclads. Within 50 years, countries were competing to build ever bigger battleships with more powerful guns. The largest of these, the American USS *Iowa* and the Japanese *Yamato*, were 270 metres long and served in the Second World War. Today, developments in missile technology have made these vast ships vulnerable and navies have replaced them with smaller, more agile vessels.

The USS Iowa *fires its guns during a display in 1984.*

The ironclad British HMS Dreadnought *was built in 1906.*

FLOATING AIR BASES

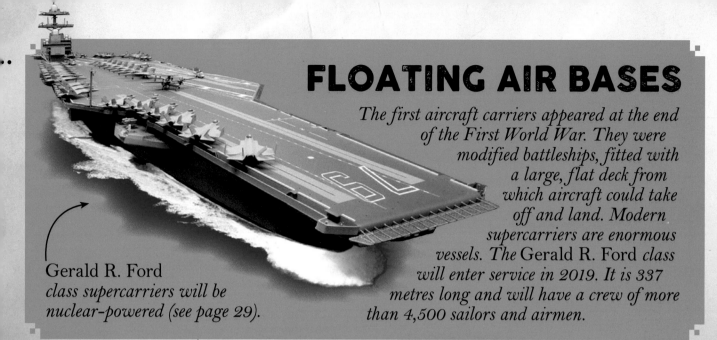

The first aircraft carriers appeared at the end of the First World War. They were modified battleships, fitted with a large, flat deck from which aircraft could take off and land. Modern supercarriers are enormous vessels. The Gerald R. Ford *class* will enter service in 2019. It is 337 metres long and will have a crew of more than 4,500 sailors and airmen.

Gerald R. Ford *class supercarriers will be nuclear-powered* (see page 29).

UNDERWATER 👉

The first attack by an underwater vessel took place during the American War of Independence (1775–1783). Built by US inventor David Bushnell, the wooden submersible *Turtle* was powered by hand cranks and designed to attach explosives to the hulls of British ships. All Bushnell's attempts to attach explosives failed, however, and the *Turtle* was not used again.

The Turtle *was powered by one man.*

25

The nuclear-powered USS Florida

🖎 MODERN SUBMARINE

Today's nuclear-powered submarines have no need to refuel. Their nuclear reactor engines allow them to stay underwater for months on end. Some carry nuclear missiles, which can deliver devastating destruction over a range of thousands of kilometres.

FLYING MACHINES

Being up in the air can be a great advantage for an attack. It provides a high viewpoint to spot enemy positions and it is the perfect place from which to launch bombs and missiles.

EARLY WAR PLANES ☛

The First World War saw rapid advances in war plane design, with Germany the first country to deploy an air force. The first attacks were from small aircraft, using bombs dropped by hand. Later, large purpose-built bombers were built. Fighter aircraft armed with machine guns were built to shoot down the bombers.

A German Albatross D-111 fighter from 1916

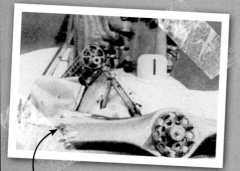

The propeller blade could be severed by a stray bullet.

FIRING POSITION

Aiming a machine gun in an early fighter aircraft was difficult. The best position for the gun was on a mount in front of the pilot, but this meant firing through the spinning propeller. To stop bullets hitting the propeller, engineers developed synchronisation gears that stopped the gun firing when a propeller blade was in the way.

AIRSHIPS

During the First World War, huge German airships filled with hydrogen gas attacked targets in the UK. They had limited success and were vulnerable to planes armed with incendiary bullets, which set fire to the hydrogen. After the war, passenger airship-building continued in Germany and in the UK, resulting in the largest flying machines ever created. However, in 1937 the German airship *Hindenburg* caught fire and crashed upon arrival in New York, killing 37 people. After that, production of airships stopped. In recent years, airships have made a small comeback, using helium gas, which doesn't catch fire, and new, ultra-light materials, such as carbon fibre.

The airship USS Macon *flies over New York City in 1933.*

27

The YB-49 was scrapped after unsuccessful tests.

FLYING WINGS

First flown in 1947, the US Northrop YB-49 was a bomber aircraft with a revolutionary design – it had no fuselage or obvious tail section. Instead every part of the plane was contained inside the wing structure that made up its body. However, the jet engines it used limited its altitude and range. As a result, the 'flying wing' project was scrapped. Fifty years later in 1997, the concept of the flying wing was reborn with the introduction of the US Northrop Grumman B-2 Spirit, or stealth bomber. The flying wing design confuses radars, making it invisible to enemy detection.

The B-2 Spirit has seen service in Iraq and Afghanistan.

ROCKETS AND LASERS

The speed and range of a rocket makes it the deadliest of all weapons. In the 20th century, rockets were developed into guided ballistic missiles. Today, they can be launched to strike a target anywhere in the world.

ROCKET POWER 👉

A rocket is a cylinder-shaped projectile powered by explosive thrust. The Chinese used gunpowder rockets as weapons against the Mongols in 1232. Early rockets were unreliable though, and were used more to scare enemy troops and horses rather than injure them.

An early Chine rocket launcher

👉 CONGREVE ROCKETS

In 1804, British engineer William Congreve developed a more reliable rocket design, using a long stick poking out of the back of the rocket to make it more stable in flight. In 1844, British inventor William Hale improved rocket design further still. He deflected the rocket's blast slightly, which caused it to spin as it flew. The spinning rocket's aim was much more accurate and it no longer needed a stick to guide it.

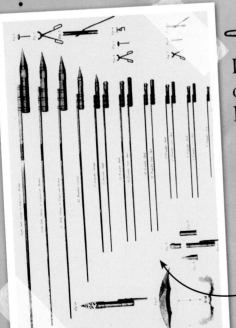

Congreve's original drawings of his rockets

☞ LONG-RANGE ROCKETS

The Second World War saw the invention of the first long-range guided ballistic missile, the German V-2. This rocket could carry a tonne of explosives and hit targets 300 kilometres away. However, its guidance system wasn't accurate and more people may have died in the slave camps used to build them than were killed by the explosives they delivered. After the war, the Russians and the US built their own long-range missiles based on the V-2.

The V-2 was the first long-range missile.

A Russian Topol-M intercontinental missile of 1997

NUCLEAR POWER ☞

At end of the Second World War, the US dropped two nuclear bombs on Japan. The bombs' power came from nuclear fission – the process of splitting atoms apart. Later devices, called thermonuclear weapons, squeeze atoms, releasing even more energy. These weapons have never been used. Today, international treaties limit the building of nuclear weapons.

A US nuclear bomb explodes over Nagasaki, Japan.

The laser weapon system on USS Ponce

LASERS

Lasers damage objects by using heat from focussed rays of light. They can blind enemy visual equipment and shoot down missiles and drones. These weapons are silent, accurate and operate at the speed of light. However, they are expensive to produce, use huge amounts of energy and can be big and cumbersome to operate. At present, they have been used on static, land-based platforms and large ships.

⊕ GLOSSARY ⊕

AMPHIBIOUS
Vehicles that can move both on land and on water.

ARTILLERY
Large guns, such as howitzers, cannons and missile launchers, which are operated by specialist crews.

CARBON FIBRE
A special material that is made up of thin strands of carbon that have been bonded together. This produces a strong but lightweight material.

FUSELAGE
The main body of an aircraft that holds the pilots, crew and any weapons or cargo.

GUNPOWDER
An explosive powder made from a mix of saltpetre, sulphur and charcoal. Gunpowder was invented in China about 1,000 years ago.

JOUSTING
A medieval sporting contest in which opponents on horseback fight with lances.

KEVLAR
A super-strong artificial fibre that can be spun into a bulletproof fabric for body armour, or made into a hard metal-like material.

LASER
A device that emits light waves that are of exactly the same frequency. The light beam from a laser stays narrow over very long distances. Powerful lasers can be used as weapons.

LEGIONARY
A soldier in the army of ancient Rome. The Roman army was divided into groups called legions.

MEDIEVAL
A period of European history that lasted from about CE 500 to 1400. Also called the Middle Ages.

MISSILE
An object that is fired at a target either by hand or from a weapon. Modern missiles may have guidance systems that allow them to seek out their target.

MUZZLE
The open end of a gun barrel.

NUCLEAR REACTOR

A device that uses radioactive material to create a controlled nuclear reaction. Modern submarines are powered by nuclear reactors, and this allows them to stay at sea for months at a time without refuelling.

PRIMER

A cap or cylinder in a bullet containing a chemical compound that ignites the charge and fires the bullet.

PROPELLER

A bladed wheel that spins around to push air or water backwards. This produces thrust to push the vehicle forwards.

PROW

The pointed front part of a ship.

RIFLE

A gun that has a grooved barrel. The grooves cause the bullet to spin, which increases the range and accuracy of the weapon.

SHELL

An explosive projectile that is fired from artillery.

SHRAPNEL

Sharp fragments from a bomb, a shell or other objects that are thrown out after an explosion.

THERMONUCLEAR WEAPONS

Powerful modern weapons that produce enormous amounts of energy by a process called nuclear fusion. This is the squeezing together of atoms so that they fuse to one another.

TRACKS

Bands of metal plates that are driven around by wheels. Tanks move along on tracks. The tracks spread the tank's weight, which stops it from sinking in soft ground.

TURRET

A rotating platform at the top of a tank that carries the gun.